The Empress of Kisses

Gwen Hart

Texas Review Press
Huntsville, Texas

Requests for permission to acknowledge material from this work should be sent to:

    Permissions
    Texas Review Press
    English Department
    Sam Houston State University
    Huntsville, TX 77341-2146

Acknowledgments:

Thank you to the editors of the following literary journals and anthologies in which these poems first appeared:
About Time, a Main Street Rag anthology: "Nostalgia"
Amethyst and Agate: Poems of Lake Superior: "Messages"
Arch & Quiver: "Origins"
Clementine Poetry Journal: "Devotion"
First Things: "The Dead Are with Us," "Eve Names the Kiss"
Measure: A Review of Formal Poetry: "Galatea Alone," "The Last Payphone"
Mezzo Cammin: "Kissing in the Rain," "Narcissus after Making Love," "To Pygmalion," "Galatea Comes to Life"
Open to Interpretation: "If Love Is Only Chemistry"
Prism International: "Only You"
The Quotable: "Early Introduction to Freud," "Flight of the Six Wild Turkeys," "Life in the Circus"
Right Hand Pointing: "Three"
The Road Not Taken: "The Empress of Kisses," "Marginalia"
The Rotary Dial: "To Summer"
Scapegoat Review: "Bat in the House," "On the Perimeter"
Silhouette Press/HCE: "If the Shoe Fits," "Your Heart Is a Rubik's Cube"
Spirit of the Horse: An Equine Anthology: "Music Education"
Valparaiso Review: "Spell"
"Galatea Alone" was anthologized in *Circe's Lament*.
"What Lips" was a finalist in the 2013 Great River Shakesepeare Festival Love Sonnet Contest.
Thank you also to Elwood Watson, the Generation X group at the Popular Culture Association, and the students in my "80s Time Machine" class for inspiring the poems in the section "Love Songs for Generation X."

Library of Congress Cataloging-in-Publication Data

Names: Hart, Gwen, 1976- author.

Title: The empress of kisses / Gwen Hart.

Description: First edition. | Huntsville, Texas : Texas Review Press, [2016]

Identifiers: LCCN 2015047407 | ISBN 9781680030891 (pbk. : alk. paper)

Subjects: LCSH: Generation X--Poetry.

Classification: LCC PS3608.A7853 A6 2016 | DDC 811/.6--dc23

LC record available at http://lccn.loc.gov/2015047407

for Roger, XOXO

Contents

I. The Empress of Kisses

II. Love Songs for Generation X

III. Kissing in the Rain

The Empress of Kisses

Spell

At school, I listened carefully all day
for novel words that I could say
when I got home. I liked to surprise my mother
with *precarious, ravishing,* or *zephyr.*
I felt the syllables fill my small
body. If I let them, words did all
the work. I didn't need to know meanings,
only sounds. Soon she would be leaning
toward me over the counter, or better yet,
pulling me to her as if we couldn't get
close enough. We'd spoon together on the couch
while I recited, delighted in her touch,
her laughter and her fingers in my hair
as I tried to find more words to keep her there.

The Empress of Kisses

Because I fell in love with poetry,
my mother sighed and said that I was doomed
to work at a cosmetics factory,
naming lipsticks. How else did I presume

to make a living? And so I buckled down:
The-only-red-umbrella-in-the-crowd,
Pearly-froth-of-a-bubble-bath-just-drawn,
Glow-of-Christmas-lights-beneath-a-shroud-

of-snow-blanketing-the-sugar-maple.
My mother scoffed. "Don't you understand
these have to fit on *tiny* lipstick labels?"
Her ridicule could not slow my hand.

I'd glimpsed my future—nothing could eclipse
a thousand kisses from a thousand lips.

Life in the Circus

My mother invented the high wire.
It started out as the clothesline.
She said my father never strung it tightly enough,
so the pants always bent into the dust, creased
as if kneeling in prayer.
She started scaling the T of the crossbar
and testing the tautness of the line
with her own weight. "If I fall and break my neck," she told him,
"it'll be your fault." Her red dress flared
above the morning glories
like an open umbrella. Before we knew it,
there were lines everywhere. She stepped carefully
over our conversations in the kitchen,
balanced only by the broom, which could be brought
down on our heads at a moment's notice.
Later she added plates piled with piping-hot food
to her routine and dared us to disturb her.
Sometimes, late at night, I woke to hear my father's
voice urging her down from the bedroom ceiling,
where she practiced walking forward and backward,
turning, and standing on one leg, a goblet of fire
trembling on the pulse-point of her delicate throat,
while he lay spread-eagle in the safety net of the bed,
sick with dizziness and desire.

Tenth Grade English

Asthmatic Mrs. Reed,
who screamed
when she sneezed
and sneezed
without warning,
refused to read
a poem straight through
without stopping
to explain the meaning.
Seized by spasms
she could not control,
she would not let
our lives be full,
uninterrupted,
lyrical.

On the Perimeter

Harold Heidegger,
who was in my gym class,
liked to think he was a car.
While we played soccer,
floor hockey, and volleyball,
he drove around
the perimeter of the gym,
shifting gears, dodging
balls and insults
from the other boys,
"Hey, Harry! Watch
where you're going!"
He never paid us much notice,
except for once
when he thrust his arm out
in a sudden signal,
turned, and ran smack into me.
The whole game stopped
while I said, "Hello, Harold,"
to which he answered,
"Beep! Beep!"
I took this to mean *I like you,*
or rather, *Quit distracting me.*
Before I could reply,
Miss Bryson blew
her whistle and yelled, "Harold!
Please stay on the road!"
He lowered his dark eyes,
backed up without a sound.

Devotion

I dug up grubs for the classroom
snake, opened the tank,
and stuck my hand right in.

I didn't flinch when he said
dissection was so fascinating
you forgot the frogs were dead.

I trapped a butterfly, a dragonfly,
a praying mantis, and a walking stick,
and stuck them through with pins.

I wrote a report on subcutaneous worms,
how doctors cut your skin and pull
them out by winding them on sticks.

Difficult? Yes. Disgusting, cruel,
but so much easier than uttering
love and following through.

Only You

I'm drawn to the man in the TV commercial
who can't cook a hotdog because he can't
boil water, but now, with a special microwavable
pouch, he can zap as many hotdogs as he wants
and have dinner ready just like that. And the boy who tries
to take out the garbage but the contents spill down
because his mother didn't buy the trash bags
with the diamond-stretch design—he could be my twin.

My mother said I shouldn't get hung up on
a specific man—I could always marry someone
like the one I'd picked. Any knock-off
brand with similar packaging would do. She didn't understand
how our hands fit together, left no space between
the fingers, and how our voices matched, off-key.
"What good is that?" she said, all this from a woman
who'd get home from the store and realize she'd
bought mild salsa, not red hot, because
she pulled jars off the shelves without looking,
the thing she really wanted always a little bit above
and to the left of what she got.

Bat in the House

He dropped like a coal
down the chimney.
Jittery and bold,
he demanded to know
where we'd hidden
the moon, where we'd shut
the sky away.
He mapped
the four corners
of the room, grimacing
up at the ceiling.
At dawn, he balled himself
into the curtains
and covered his face
with his wings.
If he couldn't have moon,
he wouldn't have sun.
All day, we drifted
like satellites
around the tight fist
of his refusal. At dusk,
we hid behind the couch
with the lights turned off
and waited for the twilight
to reel him in
through the open door.
Finally, he unfolded,
flapping like a piece
of carbon paper,
and raced up
to trace the stars,
leaving us huddled
there in the dark
with our caged
and beating hearts.

Flight of the Six Wild Turkeys

They fling themselves from nowhere
toward our car, wobbling like javelined
umbrellas. Their necks are desperate,
their feet absurd. The way they brave
the highway makes me jealous.

Oh, how tame we are in the far
right lane, my hand nowhere near
your pants, the radio mumbling on
about the weather. I strain
against the seatbelt, turn
to see them in the tamarack
as they tumble, one by one,
back into birds
and we drive sixty-five
right past the moment.

Messages

I cannot understand the language
of sand, prefixes and suffixes constantly
shifting, adhering and falling away
from the white tongues of the breakers.

All day, I watch the great ships
lumber like slow actors, forgetting
and remembering their lines
in the fog off Misery Bay.

The cottonwoods let down their
white seeds at Presque Isle Park,
forming new constellations
in the grass around our feet.

While we walk at Miner's Beach,
Petoskey stones rattle in my pocket,
narrating each step with their chatter
about the coral of long-forgotten seas.

There is no instruction manual
for setting the water on fire
the way the sun does every evening
at Copper Harbor.

A loon wets its dark beak
in the Mouth of the Huron
and writes a story
only the wind can read.

The Dead Are With Us

The dead are with us when they sing.
Though we can't see them anymore,
they sing in very little things.

They sing in clinking wedding rings,
in zippers of the clothes they wore.
The dead are with us. When they sing,

we hear their teaspoons jangling
in the corners of our kitchen drawers.
They sing in all these little things.

Their voices are not sparkling,
not melodious or pure,
but they are with us when they sing,

and we prefer that—anything!—
to silence, to the words *no more*.
We look for every little thing,

each pocket, box we can explore.
We feel them with us when they sing,
and that is not a little thing.

Marginalia

I found some comments written in my hand—
short, cryptic quips and squiggles on the page.
I wondered who I *was*, so I began

to turn the pages, trying to understand
the code—an 'X' for 'disagree'? Amazed,
I found these comments written in my hand

were tiny tickets to a foreign land,
small time machines set to a former age.
I wondered *who* I was, since I began

to see that now I love a book I panned
when I was younger. (Convictions can be changed,
I found.) The comments written in my hand

had several layers. As sediment is panned
to search for gold, I sifted through each stage,
uncovered who I was. Then I began

to pen new words. My separate selves now stand
together on the margin's narrow stage,
two sets of comments written in my hand,
connecting *who I was* and *who I am.*

Moving Alone in the Dark

All this talk of the universe expanding
makes me shrink. The auditorium
recedes around me. I see myself standing
back at my kitchen sink, my elbow numb

from reaching up to unscrew the ceiling fixture.
The light goes out every week, a flash and a pop.
I wouldn't mind if I were more dexterous
or if another bulb could slow or stop

the light from exploding, the new filament
burned thin. (I think the wiring is faulty.
The house is old, and I'm a recent tenant.)
One unlit kitchen is a minor casualty

compared to the slipping stars! The lecture over,
I walk to the arboretum, where fireflies blink,
shift, and blink. The stars are shifting slowly,
but still they shift and threaten to wink

out. I stumble in circles around the deserted park,
try to get used to moving alone in the dark.

Training the Dog

The obedience instructor says
don't forget to leave some slack
in the leash, and I think about
all the boys whose hands
I held too tightly.

The instructor says
give a command only once,
and I remember
repeating myself
to a classroom full of students
who all went home
and did the opposite
of what I'd said.

The instructor says
keep each command short
and clear, and my head reels
with the catalog of niceties
and euphemisms I employ
instead of saying the shit
I really mean.

We are working on down-stay,
and I am just about to drop
the leash and walk away,
jump in the car and drive
hundreds of miles
down the highway,
when the instructor
blows her whistle.

The dog looks up at me
with his bright eyes,
ready to try the whole routine
again, and I think about how
many times I have given up
on my dreams, and I wonder,
Will I ever, ever, ever, ever learn?

Three

American white pelicans
stood far out
in shallow water

on Storm Lake,
white feather next
to gray wing

next to orange
bill. They didn't
complain about the

wastefulness of youth.
They didn't lament
the passing of

the year. Without
any argument or
negotiation, they arranged

themselves into a
living net and
waited together on

the sand bar
for the fish
to come in.

Happiness

On a photo in a fashion magazine

I want the blue dress and the shoes, the strappy
two-toned high-heels topped with velvet bows.
If I had them, I think I would be happy.

Then, I realize the model in the snappy
convertible, the girl with the curves and upturned nose
is who I want to be. The shoes, the strappy

blue dress are bonuses, the glitzy wrapping
covering the gift of her perfect body. "Lord knows
if I were *her*," I think, "I would be happy."

In addition to her body and all the trappings,
I could use some better lighting, some make-up pros
to help me flaunt the dress and shoes, the scrappy

attitude. Wanting so much is sapping
my strength. I look out at the drying windrows.
If I were *anywhere else*, I would be happy.

I'll need the convertible, too; flapping
my hand in the breeze will banish all my lows.
I'll drive away in the blue dress, laughing, sappy-
cum-delirious. And *then* I will be happy.

Birthday Poem

Popping out of a cake
isn't all it's cracked up to be.
The sequined bathing suit
scratches your armpits,
and you get hot and sweaty
all cramped up in the dark,
waiting, night after night,
for the same old thing—
some twenty-one-year-old
grabbing at your boobs
or a geezer
in a shiny, pointed hat
about to have a heart attack.
All of the singing
starts to weigh on you,
the muffled and out-of-tune
ha-ppy birth-days.
The minutes set up
like icing, or concrete,
while you wait
huddled in that goddamned cake
until one in the morning.
Sometimes when you wake up
at noon, it happens
all over again.
You stumble
out of the sticky sheets
into the bathroom
to splash water on your face,
and when you look up,
the mirror yells
"Surprise!"

Love Songs for Generation X

X Marks the Spot

Generation X has been labeled "the forgotten generation."

Like all blank spaces
on the map, it is half-real,
half-imagined, a half-moon
of chipped thumbtack
cratering the paper
outside Boise or Stockbridge,
Tulsa or Poughkeepsie.

We know this, those of us
who have found the place,
bent up the bottom
of the torn fence, muddied
under on our bellies,
pressed a hand to the cool
concrete wall, then a cheek,
stacked six wooden
crates, and blinked into
the grimy window panes,
hoping to catch a glimpse
of the concert pulsing inside—
is it glam metal or new wave
that has been playing here,
forgotten, for decades?

We try not to breathe,
try to hold still and listen,
teetering there on the edge
of our memories,
the rotten crates
about to splinter, all of us
in one long line
holding on by our
fingertips, balanced
by the suction of a kiss.

Time Machine, 1985

I got up during
Back to the Future
to get a Coke,
and when I returned
to Theatre 2,
time had shifted,
and the same scene
was playing again
on the movie screen.
My cousins were
not in their seats,
and the earth fell away
from my feet, crushed
ice rushing down the aisle.
An usher pulled me
back to Theatre 3,
where the present
was waiting for me,
and my family
laughed me straight
into the sequel.

Challenger

What I recall
is not the fire ball,
but the principal's voice,
disembodied as God's
on the intercom, pronouncing
all the astronauts dead.
Then Shelley Marshall's mother,
who stayed home all day
watching television,
rushed into the classroom,
mascara running,
crushed her daughter
to her chest and shuffled
her out the door.
I studied my constellations
of freckles
in the restroom mirror
and did not cry.
At 3:30, I went home
on the bus, fingering
the house key hung
around my neck.
When I turned the lock,
I took a deep breath
before I pushed forward,
just like Christa McAuliffe,
Judith Resnik, and all
the other girls
who walk into the future
knowing at any moment
they might explode.

The Girls' Lavatory

The downstairs lav
was always unlocked,
crammed full
of smokers
and hairsprayers.
Fat Rachel,
"The Beast
from the East,"
liked to kick
stall doors
in on people,
so the hinges
hung, loose
or broken.

The school employed
Chad King,
my ex-boyfriend,
to paint over
the graffiti
each summer,
which he enjoyed,
since he could
always add
something new
about me.

Every year,
the lav changed
color—gray blue,
lichen green,
a whorehouse
combination of pink
with red trim.
But every year,
it looked the same—
empty paper towel
dispensers, overflowing
garbage cans, blooming
tampons in the toilets,
painted windows
sealed tightly
against escape.

Light as a Feather, Stiff as a Board

We played this game at night, when we were bored
with horror movies, truth or dare, and prank
phone calls. I was the one on the floor of the dank
basement, the body offered up on a cardboard
slab. An excellent corpse, chalky and cold,
I was praised for my stillness as my friends told
the story of my fate—the ticket sold
for the faulty roller coaster, the poison stirred
into my Coca-Cola, the man who lured
me to his car, etcetera. I bled
once, when Melissa Martin pricked
me with a pin to make sure I was dead.
I learned from that. I learned the trick:
The way to feel spectacular in death
is *not* to feel. To have no heartbeat, hold no breath.
As they lifted my body into the air,
I faded into the neither-here-nor-there.
When the game was over, I didn't hurry back;
my face remained as still as a death mask.
They shrieked and hit me with their fists,
but I gave no sign of life, not a blink or a twitch.
I was not a victim after all, but a witch,
more powerful in my absence
than I had ever been before—or since.

Music Education

When it was our choice,
we picked the songs we found
hilarious, like "Señor Dongato,"
about a cat who faints after reading
a love letter and is revived
by the smell of fish,
or "Goodbye, Old Paint."
We thought the paint was paint
on the wall, someone crying over
old chipped paint, peeling paint, cracked
green paint like the paint we picked at
when Mr. Door wasn't looking,
pulling it off the walls in long strips
or thick chips we flung at each other,
you know, paint. This was before
Jordan's mother drove her Chevy
off a cliff on purpose, before
Cheryl's sister got cancer,
long before Kim lost
the baby and Trey skidded
across the highway
on his head. We knew sorrow
about as well as we knew
horses. We thought we would
hear it coming, hoofbeats
like thunder, not like the low,
steady rhythm of the drum
in the corner, the small one
that set the tempo
for everything
we sang.

Junk Necklaces

We carried with us all the junk that we
could ever, never need, from toilet bowls
to arrows, rocket ships to sea monkeys,
harmonicas to snakes to fishing poles.
My favorites were the charms with moving parts—
the roller skate with wheels that really spun,
the baby bottle I could screw apart,
the abacus that added one plus one.
Attached to every charm were tiny bells
that shook and shimmied brightly as we walked,
so you could hear us coming down the halls
with wrenches, strawberry or chocolate malts,
alarm clocks, teacups, robots, treble clefs—
each girl a jangling world unto herself.

Surviving the Oregon Trail

Oregon Trail, the game that traumatized countless children of the '80s
and '90s is now available online for free from the Internet Archive.
– Time.com, January 2015

My brother and I drove oxen for hours that summer, taking turns
strategizing, curled up in our father's imitation leather den chair,
sucking on grape popsicles while trying to get past the non-potable water,
wagon fires, and swollen rivers. The main life lesson was that no matter
how many yokes of oxen you travel with, how many sets of clothing
and stores of food you lay by, how skilled you are at shooting
rabbits and bears, no matter if you are a banker from Boston,
a carpenter from Tennessee, a farmer from Illinois, or a sixth-grader from Ohio,
you can expect to face a number of very difficult trials: You can get stuck
for days in a blizzard, try to subsist on melted snow, burn buffalo chips for heat,
get up to let the dog out, attempt to ford the river, opt to take the toll road,
turn the air conditioning up, come down with dysentery, choke on squirrel meat,
break an axle in the mud, run out of bullets outside of Ft. Hall, hire an Indian guide,
pause to answer the phone to assure your mother you are still alive (although barely),
trade your winter clothing for more oxen, trade your oxen for more wagon wheels,
break your arm, break your other arm, break your leg, contract typhoid fever,
order a Domino's pizza, check your progress on the map, crack open
a Coca-Cola, infect your companions with typhoid fever,
try to survive on starvation rations, and, finally, come to understand
that all of your choices are like spokes in a wagon wheel leading—not
back to Independence, Missouri, or onward to Willamette, Oregon—
but straight to the heart of suburbia, where, in the end, you die,
tilted back in your father's chair, with your left hand burnt orange
from emptying a bag of Doritos, your right hand curled like a claw on the space bar,
and your bootless, sunburned heels buried deep in the wall-to-wall carpeting.

If the Shoe Fits

Their origins were humble. They could be found
at any Woolworth's, tossed in a bin, the size
magically stamped on the sole. They hit the ground
in every color—yellow to lavender, gloriously
rainbow-hued or sparkly—their beauty prized
by the fairest of them all. My feet are notoriously
too wide (my mother called them *duck feet,*
as if an evil witch had cast a spell on me),
but I wore jellies anyway, and smiled, a feat
of vanity. I walked around in agony,
hobbled by shoes no cobbler could fix,
painfully aware there was no fairy godmother,
no crystalline carriage, no fancy ball, no stepmother
to take the fall, no prince—no better life than this.

A Kiss Was a Polaroid Picture

Each one started out as flat
as a blank slate, as opaque
as a slate-gray cloud.
Slowly, shapes emerged,
blurry blocks of light
and dark. Then, colors
started to seep through, the blood
circulating now, fingertips
sharpened, electric, as the fine
lines of eyelashes drew
delicately into focus.

This is all to say
a kiss began as one
idea and became
something else. Anticipation.
Discovery. Kissers were
seekers. They would
never be satisfied
with an instant
message. Why doesn't
anyone build that brand
of kisses anymore?

Watching Molly Ringwald's Mouth

Her lips are big enough for all our dreams,
a Big Mac with cheese, and a couple Cokes.
Her mouth's a peach, split there. When she screams,

our hearts fall like college football teams
tackled in our chests. We're pink and broken.
Her lips are big enough to suck our dreams

out through our sighs. We lean in when she leans
towards the camera as if God spoke
through that breach, split air. When she screams,

her mouth's a chasm filling up the screen.
We would fall in there if we had such luck.
Her mouth is big enough to swallow dreams,

nightmares of sex we had when we were teens
pretending to be her. We wore that yoke,
mouths painted peach, split there, while we screamed.

We focus on her lips, their perfect gleam
and pucker when she pouts. We know the joke's
on us. Her lips are big. So were our dreams.
She's just the peach that splits us at the seams.

Nostalgia

"I'll *never* stop rolling my jeans,"
I declared as we got ready
for our final period of P.E.
My best friend squinted at me.
Her eyeliner was turquoise.
"You need to calm down,"
she said. But this was before
yoga or tai chi or any sort of meditation
would be taught in gym class.
We did jumping jacks and ran laps,
which made my heart pound faster.
"I'm serious," I insisted, before
the gym aide blew the whistle.
He was timing us,
comparing our scores
from the beginning
and end of the year.
I was determined to run
in circles forever, to get right
back to where I'd started,
so I could do it all again—
maybe a little bit better
this time. My friend rolled
her eyes as I shot past
her and just kept going,
reaching the finish line
before the rest of the class.
The gym aide looked
at the stopwatch,
shook his head.
"Jesus Christ," he said,
"what are you on?"

Thriller

Lamar Jackson claimed
he was Michael Jackson's cousin.
It was 1983, and I believed him,
even though we lived in Cleveland,
and I'd been to his house
with the gray asbestos siding
and the lopsided garage.
When Lamar asked me
to be his fake girlfriend
in our grade school re-enactment
of the *Thriller* video
in the gymnasium,
my heart turned
into a fistful of sequins.

Lamar grabbed my hand
and we ran for our lives,
Kangaroos sneakers squeaking
across the polished wooden floor.
We screamed as our friends,
who had become zombies
and ghouls overnight,
stumbled after us, their eyes
rolled up in their heads,
their feet dragging, but gaining
ground with every step.
I can picture us now—
a black boy and a white girl—
locking arms, turning back-to-back,
up against an angry,
encircling mob. We didn't know
what we were playing at.
We didn't know why
when they chased us down
it felt so real.

The Last Payphone

They used to come and whisper in my ear.
Their quarters, warm from pockets, slid and clinked
in one by one. They held me, called me 'dear,'

old men in ball caps and young men drunk on beer.
The teary women, soft and indistinct,
they used to come and whisper in my ear,

relay their hopes, their dreams, their joys, their fears.
Their lifeline once, now I'm all but extinct,
the last one here. They held me, all the dear

young girls—I touched their cheeks, their pierced ears.
They gossiped, giggled, gasped, and sighed in sync.
They used to come and whisper in my ear.

Their messages have faded year by year,
graffiti scrawled in earnest ballpoint ink—
Tony's the one; Just hold me; Call me, dear.

Now no one talks to me. Instead, I hear
the wind as the receiver swings, unlinked
from use. Do come. Please whisper in my ear,
cradle me, hold me close, and call me 'dear.'

Your Heart Is a Rubik's Cube

so square and cold to the touch.
I can't look away from its stoplight
colors. From certain angles, it appears
clean and whole, but rotate it,
and a little blue still mars
the red. The orange is burned
through with yellow and green.
I ask you to pass me the manual,
but you laugh and say it's not that hard:
A nine-year-old could solve it.
But a nine-year-old, not in love,
could be calm and uninvolved.
I try to channel that child,
a brown-eyed girl, who,
when presented with the colorful
contraption, would not hesitate
to take it in both hands
and twist it—*hard*—like a toy.

Early Introduction to Freud

We're gonna be speed-demons, ain't we?
said a boy I'd never seen before,
who was suddenly knee-to-knee with me,
having slid his folding chair across the floor
at driver's ed. I was fifteen,
driving slow circles in parking lots. He was eighteen,
there to get points off his license.
He sized me up with a glance,
decided he could afford to be licentious.

I opened my mouth to say *No,*
but the lights went out and the film reel
flickered. A state trooper with two gold teeth and a crooked nose
informed us that the accidents we were about to see were real.
I saw a car go over on two wheels;
I saw a head roll out from the back seat
and off to the side of the road. I didn't watch the rest.
I stared at my lap, felt the warmth of his breath
on my neck. *Hey, baby*, he said, fingers brushing my breast.
I thought, *You're hitting on me during* Highways of Death?
I wanted to push him away, but froze,
my body rigid in a corpse's pose.
I heard screams, not *my* screams, but the screams from the street-
scene, and the grill-to-grill, teeth-to-teeth force of his kiss
made my shuddering heart go something like this:
sex-and-death, sex-and-death, sex-and-death.

What Lips!

What lips these lips have kissed, and where, and why
I can recall: Behind the bowling lanes,
Lamar, who had a thing for alleys, rain,
and Lucky Strikes; then danger-seeking Cy,
who liked to lift my skirt in the supply
closet at work; then Juan, who wanted plain,
vanilla sex again and again and again.
When I think of them, I never cry.

But like the fireflies flickering in the trees,
the boys I hungered for and never won,
now *they're* a different story. They flash before
my eyes, shine brightly here, and there, and gone.
Their lips—what lips!—retain their mysteries.
No memories could make me want them more.

The Needle Jumps to Red

We assemble in the auditorium with the blood-red
curtain and the blue-backed chairs rubbed silver
from use, music stands still arranged in semi-circles
from last night's band concert. The superintendent faces
us, adjusts the microphone, speaks static,
adjusts the microphone again, and gives us the rundown:

In the event of a catastrophic explosion and shutdown
at the nuclear plant, we will evacuate according to the Code Red
plan. The high school students will be bused to (more static)
and the junior high students will be bused to the Silver
Hills Mall. All I can think about are mannequins; their faces
blurred, mutated into blank, white circles

like pale flowers or empty dinner plates. There are circular
voids in the porcelain sinks where the water goes down
the drain in the girls' lavatory. I resurface
there after deciding that I will find a hundred
places to hide, just not the mall. I run my hands under the silver
faucet, then try to tame the flyaway static

of my stand-on-end hair. At home, things remain static,
unchanged. I pretend to eat pork chops, then, while circling
the table, picking up the plates and silver-
ware, I mention Code Red to my father, who sets down
the butter. He is an engineer at the plant. He puts the bread
away. He is calm. He wants me to understand, to face

reality. He unfolds a map, smooths out the surface
on the kitchen table, the stiff paper crinkling with static
from his sleeve. He uses a compass and a colored
pencil to draw a "contamination zone." Inside this circle,
everything would be seriously affected by a meltdown:
the schools, the mall, the baseball fields. I picture a thin sliver

of moon rising, spreading its metallic silver
light over the rusted-out buses, the windowless, open-faced
buildings. Years later, talking with my Belarus student, it dawns
on me that her mother is a Priapyet survivor. The elastic
moment snaps shut around us; we are ensnared, encircled,
by an old, cold war. Hearing about her family, her cancer, feels sacred.

I want to put my palm to her face, enclose her in the circle
of my arms, feel us cinched together by history's quicksilver thread,
pins-and-needles bouncing through me like a Geiger counter's static.

The PTL Club

When donors call in their gifts,
she says their names on the air,
annunciates each one with her fingers
hinged in prayer. She talks about
giving away all of her clothes,
then buys new ones,
invests in bright eyeshadow
and brighter lipstick.
She wears a golden cross
with an inset diamond,
a matching bracelet,
and earrings. The trinkets
glitter as she talks,
throwing sparks of light
into our living rooms
from the t.v. screen.
As the prophecies
begin to crumble,
we keep watching,
noting that every time she frowns,
her foundation cracks a little,
as if an unseen auditor
is penciling in zeroes
where her eyes, mouth,
and nose used to fill up
the open ledger
of her face.

I Forgot What a Kiss Is . . .

The long-term effects
were unknown. Every week,
the Bears beat people up
on television, and every week
we *almost* had sex.
Madonna tried to warn us
in that video where she gets
amnesia, puts on a white dress,
and believes she's a virgin again.
Now we all have some version
of that song running through our heads,
and we say things like
I don't even remember going out with him!
That's because a kiss is
a concussion. Repeated exposure
disrupts brain functions. If you interrupt
my story to ask *Which guy*
are we talking about? I can start
to count backwards on my fingers,
then lose track and wonder,
What year is it, and how many
feelings am I holding up?

November 9th, 1989

For thirty years there is no kiss.
Then there is the possibility of a kiss,
like a rumble or a half-heard shout—
did it come from this side
or that side? When the kiss
breaks through, we all struggle
to register the impossible,
how the wall came down,
how their lips found each other,
every obstacle reduced to rubble
around their feet, the bright paint
of her lipstick smeared,
unintelligible graffiti all over
the changed angles of his face.

Anniversary Track

My heart
is a cassette tape
that's been played
and rewound, played
and rewound, sped up
and slowed down,
the best bits sought out
again and again
until all the delicate
darkness unravels
in kinks and snarls
on the Chevy's floorboard.
My love is a bad track
that can't be played back
until it's spooled back
into tight, compact blackness,
carefully, delicately,
by hand with a pencil:
Your hand, your pencil.

Kissing in the Rain

Kissing in the Rain

is overrated, claims my jaded student.
"I know someone who *tried* it," says another,
rolling her eyes. I picture a couple, heads bent
together, no umbrella. They're getting wetter

by the second. His shirt is plastered against
his chest, and her mascara's turned to ink
and drawn calligraphy down her cheek. The fence
they lean on bends and sways—yet they don't think

it's overrated. Their lips are warm, the rain
is cool. His hand is sliding inside her dress.
My students have moved on. Now they complain
a swimming pool is no place to have sex.

"Just *think* about it," they insist, winking.
I know two hours from now I'll still be thinking.

To Summer

They said it wouldn't last. You liked to turn
the thermostat to ninety, take off all
your clothes and stand under the "waterfall"
in the shower stall until you drained the cistern.

At first I hoped that you could change, could learn
to bundle up in sweaters, enjoy the fall.
And then I found you curled up in a ball
around a candle, nose and fingers burned.

The days grew short; the nights were getting longer.
There were some tough decisions to be made.
I bought the ticket, drove you and your belongings
(Speedo, sunblock, shades) to J.F.K.

At least I got a postcard—*I belong here!*
Thank you, darling—postmarked Adelaide.

Drought Sonnet

The sky is dry. No course can satisfy
the clouds. They drift and shrink, reverse and twist,
like cobwebs scattered by the slightest sigh.
(I can't forget the hour of our last kiss.)

The earth is burned. No gardener's gentle touch
can make the bulbs unshrivel in their beds.
The roses died without a sound, fists clenched.
(Remember how they opened, pinks and reds?)

The stream is starved, a hieroglyphic carved
into the clay. It reads: a ribbon ran
along this path, shiny, cool, and curved.
(We waded in the water, hand-in-hand.)

The world is wrecked without rain's wizardry.
(If only you would hurry back to me).

Eve Names the Kiss

He sat upon the garden wall.
She had her fingers on his knees.
The smallest leaves began to fall.
A subtle difference in the breeze

prompted the tiger and the hare
to linger there. Even the snake
slithered closer so to hear
what sound she'd make. They'd heard him speak

a thousand times, define the world
from bumblebee to elephant.
His syllables were muscled, bold.
But she, they felt, was different.

The future trembled on her lips.
Her mouth was like an apple, split,
two halves as supple as her hips.
And when she said the word, he bit.

Origins

We're just the raw material
heaped on the bed, a knot of flesh
fired in the sheets, combustible.
A flare that goes off in one flash,

a cymbal crash, mysterious
first source of rushing waterfall.
We've no control. Love chooses us;
we're just the raw material.

Love Note for Clark

Some people have a thing for Superman.
Not me. I'm partial to Clark Kent.
It's the ordinary glasses in the hands

that can bend steel, the draping of the bland
suit over biceps that were meant
to throw people. It's one thing for Superman

to swoop in and save the day, reprimand
the bad guys with a glance, but the pent-
up fire behind the ordinary glasses, the hands

that can catch bullets clutching a pencil, land-
ing a story. That gets me. Clark does what Superman can't—
so many people have this thing for Superman

that he doesn't dare join the community band
or squeeze tomatoes at the supermarket.
The power's in the ordinary glasses that he hands

over in the one-shot phone booth striptease, sans
them he's just his alter-ego, man of blue and red flint.
Some people have a thing for Superman.
I like my extra and my ordinary hand-in-hand.

To Pygmalion

It's easy to love a woman who doesn't move
or make a face or threaten to just walk
right out that door, who doesn't have to prove
she's going to the grocery store and back—
that's all. It's easy when she doesn't talk
or sigh or whimper, easy to believe
you know exactly what she'd like, to gawk
up at her breasts and shoulders, at the stone
you've carved to look like other girls you've known,
their curves perfected now, rendered—minus
the moles and scars—with an alabaster knife.
You sob and clutch her waist, praying to Venus,
who hears your plea for a soft and supple wife,
and pities Galatea, grants her life.

Galatea Comes to Life

I couldn't breathe. His lips were on my lips,
his tongue was in my mouth—his hair, my nose—
the tangle so complete—his hands, my hips—
I couldn't free myself or break the pose

he'd carved me in. Then he lost his grip,
stumbled backwards, looked at me and froze.
I sucked in air, my stomach doing flips.
Cautiously, he inspected me up-close,

gently circling his fingertips
around my navel, down to my thighs, my toes.
He said we should get married, hurried to slip
my arm in a sleeve, button up my clothes.

He took my hand. He said we had to go.
I learned to say yes before I could say no.

Galatea Alone

I have grown accustomed to his hands,
the rough palms on my knees, the cracked thumbs
still caked with plaster making their demands,
circling my thigh until it's numb.

And I have grown accustomed to his praise.
I stand before his friends, unpin my hair,
arrange my arms, and lower my gaze
so he can boast that no one else compares.

But I am still adjusting to the feeling
that these long limbs are more than a display.
(The velvet of my skin can send me reeling
when I bathe!) Oh, Venus, let him stay

out late, tell his stories, drink his wine.
Tonight, let this body be all mine.

Galatea and the Kicking Foot

We lie together in the tub, the curve
my belly makes emerging like the moon
in front of us. Pygmalion worked to carve
my waist, to make it slender. As we spoon,
I sense his disappointment in his 'ruined'
artwork, all his precious lines undone.

He is a fool. I'm doubling now, and soon
I will be two instead of one. Not stone,
but flexible, creative, my womb has grown
to cradle what is budding in me right
out of my blood and muscle, flesh and bone.

I feel a twinge, a tremor of delight,
a kicking foot! For this, I thank you, Venus:
to love the shapes of life is woman's genius.

Narcissus after Making Love

He inhales a sweetness, there at the back of her neck.
It's not perfume; he knows she never wears
any. So what is it that he detects—
a powder? No, nor pomade in her hair.

He investigates her cheeks, her breasts, her arms,
even her knees and ankles prick his nose.
The aroma's subtle, magical, and warm—
not honeysuckle, lavender, or rose.

What garden has she walked through? What strange blossom
has she picked? He bends again to kiss
her neck, and begs her, "Tell me what this custom
potion is, this fragrance I can't resist?"

She laughs at him, his nose pressed to her skin:
"It's only your own scent, you fool, rubbed in."

Enough

The roses that you sent me were so plush
I thought that they would never lose their blush.
But even though I watered, trimmed, and fussed,
they shriveled in the vase and turned to dust.

The Chevy that we paid for, newly buffed
to shine so bright, could never turn to rust.
We drove it through ten winters' salt and slush,
then towed it to the junkyard, had it crushed.

And what, then, has become of all our lust?
The flames were fanned to fever by a gust
of wind so swift and hot it seemed to rush
the blaze to turn to ash, as fires must.

Desire burns away. But love's not lust.
Love's forged in fire, and made of stronger stuff.
When flowers fade and cars succumb to rust,
it's love that blooms afresh and carries us.

If Love Is Only Chemistry

a double sonnenizio on a line by Kim Addonizio

Guess what. If love is only chemistry
then there's a secret formula, a love
potion that starts it all, the lover's
hand on another's lovely thigh,
all the waiting-to-be-loved parts
of the body on fire, loving the suspense
as much as they'd love to jump
to the front of the line. Who mixes love up
in what remote factory, and what kind of gloves
must they wear to keep the love from
soaking into their skin, making them slovenly,
too foolish to work, making love on the night
shift in a room that smells like clover or rye,
love's byproducts burning a bright red flame in the sky?

Let's drive all night, looking for love's guards at the gates,
drive without headlights while the moon makes love
to the gravel roads, loving each curve
that might lead us closer, each lovely shoulder
where we might pull over and talk
or kiss, my knee on the glove compartment,
your hands as soft and familiar as the love songs
playing on LUV radio. We'll drive slowly
and kiss slowly, foxgloves dripping like torn hearts
outside the building marked L.O.V.E.
DO NOT ENTER, where they quarantine the lovesick,
the love-formula-contaminated workers and the people
like us who discover love's headquarters under cover
of night, twist open the valves, and wake up lovers.

Acknowledgments:

Thank you to the editors of the following literary journals and anthologies in which these poems first appeared:

About Time, a Main Street Rag anthology: "Nostalgia"

Amethyst and Agate: Poems of Lake Superior: "Messages"

Arch & Quiver: "Origins"

Clementine Poetry Journal: "Devotion"

First Things: "The Dead Are with Us," "Eve Names the Kiss"

Measure: A Review of Formal Poetry: "Galatea Alone," "The Last Payphone"

Mezzo Cammin: "Kissing in the Rain," "Narcissus after Making Love," "To Pygmalion," "Galatea Comes to Life"

Open to Interpretation: "If Love Is Only Chemistry"

Prism International: "Only You"

The Quotable: "Early Introduction to Freud," "Flight of the Six Wild Turkeys," "Life in the Circus"

Right Hand Pointing: "Three"

The Road Not Taken: "The Empress of Kisses," "Marginalia"

The Rotary Dial: "To Summer"

Scapegoat Review: "Bat in the House," "On the Perimeter"

Silhouette Press/HCE: "If the Shoe Fits," "Your Heart Is a Rubik's Cube"

Spirit of the Horse: An Equine Anthology: "Music Education"

Valparaiso Review: "Spell"

"Galatea Alone" was anthologized in *Circe's Lament*.

"What Lips" was a finalist in the 2013 Great River Shakespeare Festival Love Sonnet Contest.

Thank you also to Elwood Watson, the Generation X group at the Popular Culture Association, and the students in my "80s Time Machine" class for inspiring the poems in the section "Love Songs for Generation X."

Gwen Hart teaches writing at Buena Vista University in Storm Lake, Iowa. She holds an M.A. in Creative Writing from Hollins University, an M.F.A. from Minnesota State University, and a Ph.D. in Rhetoric and Composition from Ohio University. She is the author of several chapbooks and the poetry collection Lost and Found (David Robert Books). She is a Generation Xer and a regular contributor to the Popular Culture Association Conference.